CW01163788

ABOUT WOODBURY PARK CEMETERY

"This resting-place is beautifully laid out as a mortuary garden. Shrubs, trees, evergreens, moss-covered graves and sculptured tombs impart to it a pleasing aspect".

So said a nineteenth century town guide about Woodbury Park Cemetery. Now Grade II Listed, it is today also a site of special nature conservation interest.

Opened in 1849 to take over from the overflowing graveyard of Holy Trinity as Town Cemetery, it was finally closed in 1934. Over 6000 people lie here ranging from rich merchants to workhouse children. Its 640 memorials record many who made their mark locally, and some nationally and internationally.

The Friends of Woodbury Park Cemetery were established in 2006 to conserve and enhance this heritage site for the public to enjoy, to research its memorials, to protect its rare plants and smaller wildlife and to encourage its use as an educational resource. You can find out more about our activities and projects on our website fwpc.org.uk. We warmly welcome all who would like to get involved in any aspect of this work.

About the author

This booklet by David Bushell is one of a series by our members telling the stories of some of those buried here. He read history at the University of Leicester and has worked in commercial and trade association insurance for thirty years and in governance and related roles at a medical royal college before recent retirement. He is currently the Pugin Society Hon. Secretary.

Illustrations:

Front cover: tondo of Sydney Smirke

Back cover: traditional architect instruments

ISBN 978-1-911650-16-4

Sydney Smirke 1797-1877
An honourable, cultivated and accomplished architect

Contents

Smirke Genealogical Tables

1. Introduction

2. The Smirke Tomb in Woodbury Park Cemetery

3. The Smirke Family and Early Years

4. Grand Tour

5. Patronage, Clubs and Institutions

6. Marriage and Children

7. Town Planning and Water Supplies

8. Later Career and Academic Duties

9. Folkestone

10. Tunbridge Wells

Sources and some local places to visit Smirke's architectural work

Family of Robert Smirke (1753–1845)

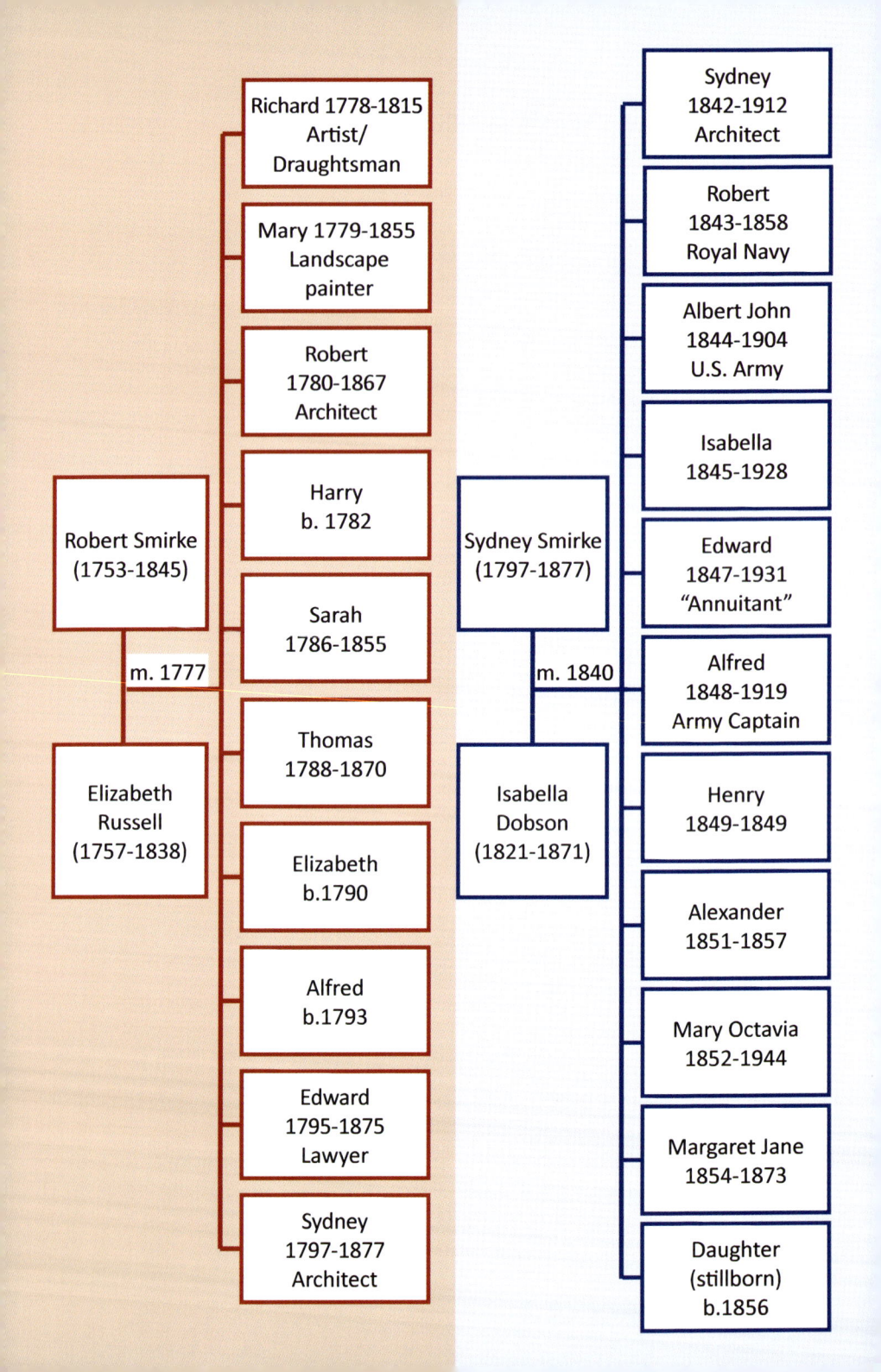

Robert Smirke (1753–1845) m. 1777 **Elizabeth Russell (1757–1838)**

Children:
- Richard 1778–1815, Artist/Draughtsman
- Mary 1779–1855, Landscape painter
- Robert 1780–1867, Architect
- Harry b. 1782
- Sarah 1786–1855
- Thomas 1788–1870
- Elizabeth b. 1790
- Alfred b. 1793
- Edward 1795–1875, Lawyer
- Sydney 1797–1877, Architect

Sydney Smirke (1797–1877) m. 1840 **Isabella Dobson (1821–1871)**

Children:
- Sydney 1842–1912, Architect
- Robert 1843–1858, Royal Navy
- Albert John 1844–1904, U.S. Army
- Isabella 1845–1928
- Edward 1847–1931, "Annuitant"
- Alfred 1848–1919, Army Captain
- Henry 1849–1849
- Alexander 1851–1857
- Mary Octavia 1852–1944
- Margaret Jane 1854–1873
- Daughter (stillborn) b. 1856

1. Introduction

Sydney Smirke was a leading architect of the early and mid Victorian era and many – although not all – of his creations and restorations can still be seen today. The product of an established architectural and artistic family he benefited from his lineage and the many connections and patronages that propelled his career into the first rank of achievement. Based in London, his work took place in many parts of the country including Kent, in Folkestone. As with many achieving Victorians who chose a seaside resort or inland spa for retirement, Smirke spent the last eight of his 80 years in Tunbridge Wells. This publication outlines his life and career, emphasising the personal more than the professional which is covered more extensively and expertly elsewhere.

A note on the state of architectural training in England in the late 18th and early 19th centuries. Records in the Dictionary of National Biography indicate a very varied background and training at this time although most aspiring architects came from the middle classes and two-thirds, rising to three quarters by the second quarter of the 19th century, were apprenticed to a practising architect. Private study and travel also helped to inform aspiring architects. Formal professionalisation emerged with the founding of the Royal Institute of British Architects in 1834 with later reforms to protect the title of architect such as via the Architects (Registration) Act of 1931.

The Smirke brothers trained by way of the Royal Academy Schools which taught architecture until the 1950s. Aspiring architects entering the Schools were always in a minority compared to painters and sculptors. The curriculum for architecture students was very different from the other RA students, being exempt from drawing classes but expected to be attached to established architectural practices as pupils and attending the RA library in the evenings for private study. There was also compulsory attendance at the annual course of six architectural lectures, given in Smirke's time by Sir John Soane, the RA's Professor of Architecture from 1806 to 1837.

2. The Smirke Tomb in Woodbury Park Cemetery

Smirke Tomb – Woodbury Park Cemetery, Tunbridge Wells

Tombs are the clothes of the dead; a grave is but a plain Suit, and a rich monument is one embroyder'd – Revd Thomas Fuller (1608-61), *The Holy State and the Profane State,* 1642.

This ornate tomb, contrasting with the typically unadorned memorials in Tunbridge Wells' Woodbury Park Cemetery, stands high on the northern promontory surrounded by fellow achievers and benefactors of the mid Victorian age.

It was designed by Smirke's architect friend, John Loughborough Pearson, most famous for his church building in particular the cathedral for the newly established diocese of Truro. Smirke commissioned it for his youngest daughter, Margaret Jane, who died of enteric fever (typhoid) and pneumonia on 29 November 1873 while staying in Brighton. No doubt he also planned that he would join his daughter so it may be speculated that the symbolism it carried also represented his own professional and philanthropic interests and his grief at losing his younger unmarried daughter, a companion in his old age in Tunbridge Wells following the death of his wife in 1871.

The tomb was described by a former employee of Pearson as set out in Antony Quiney's 1978 book on Pearson's works. The mausoleum as it was termed was a tomb chest with overhanging cruciform roof with gables to ends and arms, carried by stout red Devonshire columns with foliated capitals; exposed sides of chest have inscriptions or symbols within cusped foils. The columns may reflect Smirke's interest in classical architecture but in masonic terms refer to the two great pillars standing at the entrance to King Solomon's temple at Jerusalem. The tomb also sports some Stars of David or Hexalpha, used by Christians, Jews and Masons and may remind posterity of Smirke's benevolent deeds, in particular his founding of and long association with the Architects' Benevolent Fund. The Classic lines of the tomb remind us of his variation of classical architecture. The four pink granite polished pillars (the Friends of Woodbury Park Cemetery had paid local stonemasons Burslems to replace one that was missing) can be seen to represent his introduction of polished granite pillars to England as evidenced in his work at the Carlton Club, inspired by Jacob Sansovino's Library of St Mark's, Venice, with its long façade facing the Doge's Palace. Considered Sansovino's masterpiece and a key work in Venetian Renaissance architecture, the sixteenth century building was described as perhaps the richest and most ornate building that there has been since ancient times up until now. More prosaically, the acanthus motifs adorning the tomb echo Greek and Roman antiquities as well as their association with virginity and the prickly journey from life to death and on to the ultimate triumph of eternal life while the marguerites represent innocence, purity and love. In numerology, the marguerite is associated with the number seven which represents spiritual awakening, intuition and inner wisdom and can be a sign that one is being called to embark on a spiritual journey.

John Loughborough Pearson courtesy of NPG

3. The Smirke Family and Early Years

Sydney Smirke was was one of a large family of siblings, being the last of ten children when he was born in London on 20 December 1797 and baptized on 14 January 1798 at St Pancras Old Church. He was the seventh son of Robert Smirke (1753-1845) and Elizabeth Smirke, nee Russell (1757-1838), daughter of John and Judith Russell. They had married in 1777. Robert was a painter and illustrator, a member of the Royal Academy, born in Wigton near Carlisle, the son of a travelling artist. His career was not helped by his revolutionary political opinions expressed in his series of satirical Catalogues Raisonnes lampooning the great and good of British art patronage. He died at 3 Osnaburgh Terrace, Regent's Park, London on 5 January 1845 aged 92 and is buried in Kensal Green cemetery.

Of Smirke's many siblings, three brothers became well known as did sister Mary, a landscape painter and translator, who had exhibited six paintings at the Royal Academy between 1809 and 1814. Another sister, Sarah went on to marry Samuel Baker, a building contractor operating in Rochester and London. The three better known brothers were firstborn Richard, an antiquarian draughtsman and artist who had been educated at the Royal Academy Schools and received a gold medal for a picture of Samson and Delilah in 1799; Sir Robert, architect and Smirke's mentor and apprentice master (more of him below); and Sir Edward, a lawyer, expert on forensic and documentary law

Robert Smirke
Courtesy of NPG

and a member of the Royal Archaeological Institute living in London and the west country. A Cambridge graduate called to the bar at Middle Temple in 1824, Edward was on the western circuit and the Hampshire sessions. He was solicitor general to the Prince of Wales from December 1844, promoted to attorney general in 1852, a post he held to 1870 when he retired from all his official positions and received a knighthood. He also picked up the posts of Vice-warden of the Stannaries of Cornwall and Devon (1853-1870) and Recorder of Southampton (1846—1855). He died at 18 Thurloe Street, South Kensington on 4 March 1875 and is also buried at Kensal Green cemetery. Smirke's other siblings were Harry; Thomas; Elizabeth; and Alfred.

Sir Robert Smirke
Courtesy of NPG

Surrounded by family members who were artists and architects, Smirke's interest in art and design could be considered innate. He was sent to Eywood, the Herefordshire seat of the Harleys, where he studied under a private tutor with Lord Oxford's eldest son. Aged 18, he transferred to his elder brother, Robert's, office as an articled pupil, simultaneously joining the Royal Academy Schools where he won the Gold Medal in 1819 with a drawing of "Pliny's Villa". Smirke then spent several years travelling on and off in Europe, in particular Italy and Sicily, studying the local antiquaries and architecture.

4. Grand Tour

As had been the fashion for men of means in the late eighteenth century to round off their education yet restricted by war with the French revolutionaries and Napoleon Bonaparte, but revived after Waterloo, Smirke undertook European travels over several years. One Grand Tour of Europe was undertaken aged 26, departing in September 1824 and lasting some 18 months, ending in February 1826. The Royal Institute of British Architects archives deposited at the Victoria & Albert Museum contain a collection of his many letters home – mainly to his father, but also to brothers Robert and Edward. They provide an interesting insight into a young person's travels at that time, noting his experiences in accommodation and food, as well as thoughts on the architecture he encountered. It was not his first foreign trip however, as in 1819 Smirke won the Gold Medal and Travelling Scholarship as a student of the Royal Academy Schools and the following year visited Italy, including Rome and Sicily.

Notre Dame Paris
Photo by Sebastien on Unsplash

In a letter from Paris to his father dated 30 September 1824, Smirke noted that *it is calculated that one sixtieth of the whole population of Paris go to the theatre every night* while he took delight in the variety and reasonableness of Parisian restaurant food: *my dinners are amazingly cheap with a choice of eight soups, choice of a long list of meats, turbot or carp and dessert of fruits with a half bottle of wine or a whole bottle of porter for two francs.*

But his accommodation was less to his liking both in St Denis and Paris where he was not sleeping alone but for a *multitude of fleas regaled themselves on me every night*. His response was to camphor himself all over when going to bed.

He travelled on via Dijon to Genoa, where, on being asked by his father as to his health, responded that he was *perfectly well – I don't know why I should not be, for I live with perfect regularity and am breathing sea air in a genial climate*. He left Genoa *with a very favourable impression of the place although it is not in the least like the town I had imagined*. Commenting on Genoa's architecture, *the guide books are constantly reminding me of Paff's auctioneering advertisements … but the Palaces are grand although many are in a complete state of decay*. However, again his accommodation caused him concern: *I took my post in the Pension Sevifix which was represented to me as one of the cleanest, second rate inns – clean, however is a relative term and my offended senses are unanimous in pronouncing it foul, though in this land of filth, it may be considered tidy*. He sought new lodgings, recommended by the Secretary to the English Minister, for five francs a week noting *here I am in a room 13 by 24 of a handsome height and well furnished. I have the whole family by turn to wait on me, consisting of a host (a tailor), his spouse, two daughters and a little son, they none of them speak French but the tailor himself.*

By December 1824 Smirke had reached Rome. He noted the civility of the people but it was *almost bare of architectural attractions – at least for me – for the almost universal style of the buildings that pretend to any importance is of that semi-gothic kind which unfortunately prevailed so much in Italy when Italy was most able to build*. He went on to comment: *my impressions about Rome – though not struck by some things and quite disappointed in others – I can say with great positiveness that, in the main, the city goes far beyond my expectations*. Regarding St Peter's Basilica in the Vatican, *I can only repeat the often-told story of its ugly front and mismanaged proportions… yet … the interior is one of those things one thanks one's stars that one has seen.*

The Collisseum Rome

Travelling in Milan Smirke wrote home to report *I find Milan a very large, gay and highly polished city, with a great deal for an idle visitor to do, but very little for a busy one (in the way of architecture): there are six or seven theatres open every night and the cafés vie with those of Paris for glass and polished marble, but the architecture of the place is below par.* Venice improved his opinion of Italy however: *I have left Italy with very agreeable impressions, for my stay at Venice has afforded me much enjoyment.*

December 1825 saw Smirke in Vienna about which he concluded *a stay which is not compensated by the discovery of any architectural beauties in this city and whatever natural beauties there may be are lost in the mists which are always one of the peculiarities of a Sirocco wind.*

Returning home via Bavaria, the Rhine, Cologne and finally Brussels, Smirke noted from Munich that *the King of Bavaria is animated by a laudable zeal for architecture and is causing almost a new city to grow up around him.*

Many years later, on 5 November 1860, Smirke was to regale his thoughts and experiences in Sicily to an ordinary general meeting of RIBA (*published in the RIBA Transactions 1st series 11 1860-61*). He noted that while Sicily had so many objects of archaeological and artistic interest, it attracted few tourists. In his view that was because *the island lies out of the ordinary track of tourists; it offers but few of the facilities for internal travelling found in most other countries of Europe, and, therefore, cannot be traversed without a good deal of personal inconvenience. The inns are, for the most part, wretchedly bad, and often altogether wanting; bridges are few in number, and roads often mere mule-tracks.*

In his lecture, Smirke noted Sicily's richness in the remains from the Phoenician, Greek, Roman, Arabic, Norman and Medieval periods, *with untold wealth in flax, timber, sulphur, marble and many other natural products only awaiting the capitalist and merchant.* He listed seven types of marble and eighteen varieties of jasper as examples of his admiration for the natural resources found in Sicily

Palermo by Cristino Gottardi on Unsplash

5. Patronage, Clubs and Institutions

Returning from his extensive Mediterranean travels in 1827, Smirke found a position as a Clerk of the King's Works which required impartiality in ensuring that value for money for the client - rather than the contractor - is achieved through rigorous and detailed inspection of materials and workmanship throughout the building process. After five years the Office of Works was reorganised and his post abolished. But his career continued as assistant and heir to his brother, Robert's, practice, both benefitting from Tory patronage. Brother Robert's significant patrons were the Earl of Lonsdale and Sir Robert Peel, Prime Minister 1834-35 and 1841-46. Smirke designed Peel's new portrait gallery at his seat, Drayton Manor, Staffordshire and the Grammar School at Tamworth, in Peel's Parliamentary constituency. His work with the Lonsdales began on their Whitehaven estate and in Rutland. Further patronage came from other Tories and from the nominally Whig 13th Earl of Derby whose son had succeeded Peel as leader of the Tory party. Many commissions here took place in Lancashire, including alterations at Knowsley Hall, hotel, and assembly rooms at Bury, rectories and small churches. Smirke gradually built up a flourishing and wide-ranging practice although only 80 commissions have been discovered, far fewer than some contemporaries. Even so, his career made him a rich man, leaving some £80,000 at his death (equivalent to £12 million today). His range included private houses and churches, public buildings (such as Custom Houses at Bristol, Newcastle, Shoreham, and Gloucester), suburban developments (The Park, Ealing and Lord Radnor's estate at Folkestone – see below), institutional and public works.

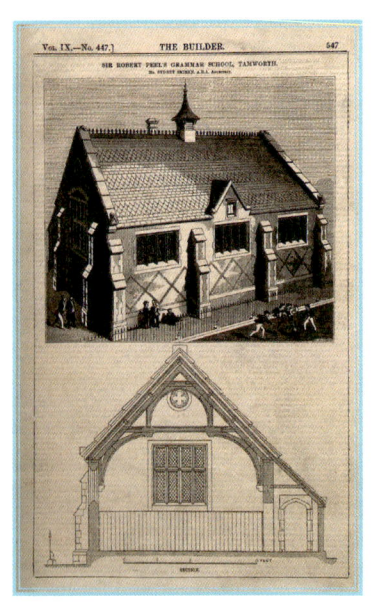

Sir Robert Peel's Grammar School Tamworth

Of prominence in their architectural careers, the Smirke brothers designed a few London clubs. Sydney's contribution was the Oxford and Cambridge Club (working with brother Robert), the old Conservative Club in St James's Street (jointly with George Basevi, a relative of Disraeli) and the second Carlton Club in Pall Mall. Smirke was best known for designing the circular reading room at the British Museum in 1857, used as the main reading room of the British Library until its move to St Pancras in 1997. The space today is now used for exhibitions. His other early and mid-career works included shopping arcades at the Oxford Street Pantheon (1833-34) (demolished in favour of the Marks & Spencer HQ) and the Exeter Change in The Strand (1843-44); restoration of York Minster's nave roof (1841) and canopies to the chapter house seats (1844-5); the dome chapel of the Bethlem Royal Hospital (now housing the Imperial War Museum) (1846); and the Frewen Mausoleum at St Mary's Church, Northiam (1846). Smirke was also an adviser or competition judge for other buildings including the London Smallpox Hospital (1848), the Industrial School at Feltham (1856) and London's Langham Place Hotel (1862). In 1861 he was one of a small group of advisers forming a committee appointed by the Palace of Westminster's Chief Commissioner to consider the best means of preserving the stones of the Palace.

New Dome Bethlem Hospital
Illustrated London News 15 Feb 1845
ILN Hist Archive Gale

Carlton Club 1932

*Union Club by
Sir Robert Smirke*

*Oxford and Cambridge
Club London*

Patronage was augmented by club membership as a means of mixing with one's peers, whether friend or rival, sometimes both. Both Smirke and George Basevi became honorary members of the Conservative Club after completing their new build in 1845 while earlier, in 1838, Smirke had been elected a member of the Athenaeum Club, built to the design of Decimus Burton, with whom he had collaborated (restoration of the Temple Church) and competed (Burton had been asked to negotiate for a site for the Conservative Club but was overlooked when the build commission was given to Smirke). The original membership cap had been set at 1,000 but 400 more were needed to increase income. Anyone seeking Athenaeum Club membership usually had to wait many years before election but to increase the membership numbers, 40 were elected in 1838. This proved controversial and those elected then were referred to informally as the "Forty Thieves". Those joining with Smirke (whose name had been down for membership since 1834) included such luminaries as Charles Darwin, Charles Lyell, Henry Holland and Charles Dickens. As the club's architect, Decimus Burton had been admitted into membership previously, in 1835. Smirke's proposer and seconder for membership were Sir Thomas Phillipps, Bart (antiquary and book collector) and Sir Henry Ellis (Principal Librarian, British Museum, joint secretary, Society of Antiquaries and founder, Royal Numismatic Society) respectively. Smirke's friend, the eminent architect John Loughborough Pearson entered the club's candidate book in 1874 (nominated no less than by the eminent church architect George Edmund Street and the Archbishop of Canterbury) but had to wait until 1887 before election. Proposers and/or seconders could easily have died before their candidate was elected when substitutes were found. In this case by 1887 Edward White Benson was Archbishop of Canterbury, formerly the first Bishop of Truro who started work on building a cathedral at Truro whose architect, as we have noted, was John Loughborough Pearson.

It is not known how often Smirke frequented the Athenaeum but in 1865 he did propose for membership an architect, Edward Henry Martineau of 30 Weymouth Street, Portland Place, London (finally admitted in 1880). The correspondence records of the club are focussed on complaints, the complainants putting comments on the back of dining bills. While none have been found from Smirke the content of others may provide amusement today: slow service, coffee of inferior quality. The Bishop of Oxford (Samuel Wilberforce, son of William) on two occasions in 1860 complained: *served Potage Julien instead of mutton broth and no shrimp sauce to be had...rump steak so tough it could not be swallowed*. Back in 1849 a Mr D Jardine complained the *partridge in this case was not larger than a sparrow and was utterly insufficient for any diner...I ordered cold beef to supplement the deficiency and I object to being charged six pence for it.*

Another popular association with architects and builders is Freemasonry. Although no evidence has been found to suggest Smirke was a Freemason, others close to him were, or became masons after his death. His older brother, Sir Robert Smirke became a mason as early as 1808, initiated into the prestigious Lodge of Antiquity No. 2. He was living in The Albany, London at that time and it was also in that year that the Duke of Sussex joined the lodge (elected Grand Master in 1813). Two of Smirke's sons became masons: his namesake Sydney, initiated into St Margaret's Lodge No. 1872 on 16 January 1902 (resigned in 1910); Albert John joining the Prince of Wales Lodge No. 1003 on 2 August 1871, meeting at Jersey, Channel Islands. He was registered as being "from Spain". And the designer of Smirke's tomb, John Loughborough Pearson, was not a mason when he knew Smirke but became one on 26 March 1880 when he was initiated into The Jerusalem Lodge No. 197. Pearson was described as an architect living at 46 Harley Street, London.

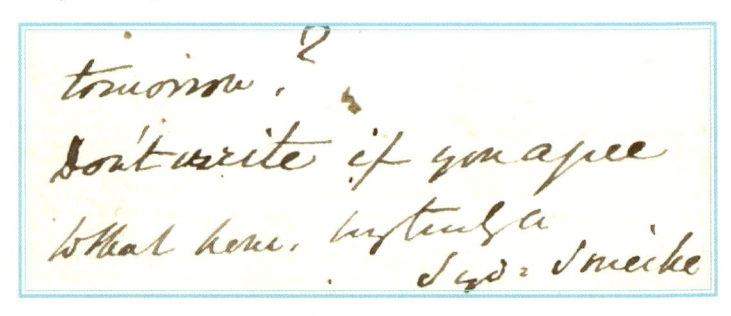

example of Smirke's handwriting

6. Marriage and Children

Not uncommon amongst professional men of the time, Smirke did not marry until he was almost 43, on 8 December 1840. His wife was Isabella Lange Dobson (1821-71), eldest daughter of John Dobson (1787-1865) and Isabella Rutherford (died 1846). As with many marriages within the professional and gentry classes, John Dobson was not unknown to the Smirke family. Born in Newcastle -upon-Tyne to a successful market gardener, Dobson eventually trained in Newcastle as an architect but not before spending some time in London studying watercolour and becoming friendly with Robert Smirke and his sons, Robert and Sydney. John based his large and varied architectural practice in Newcastle, finally being admitted as a Fellow of RIBA in 1845, his sponsors including Sydney Smirke who had received his own fellowship the previous year. The family connections continued into the next generation as Smirke's wife's brother, Alexander, trained as an architect under Smirke although he was subsequently killed in an explosion in Gateshead in October 1854, aged only 25. In her memoir of her late father, Isabella's sister, Margaret Jane Dobson stated this about her father: *In the early part of his career he also formed the friendship of his future son-in-law, Sydney Smirke, R A; an intimacy which grew with years, and was life-long. During the whole of this protracted period they were constantly in the habit of consulting one another, comparing notes, and exchanging sketches. The correspondence, so full of interest in an architectural point of view, is unfortunately lost, the few letters that now remain being only of a trivial nature. This is truly to be regretted.*

Smirke in middle age
Ilustrated London News 10 Dec 1859
ILN Hist Archive Gale

The marriage produced seven sons and three daughters (and one stillborn daughter, at Isabella's last confinement in March 1856). The eldest child, Sydney, became an architect and artist. Articled to his father between 1855 and 1862, then moving to the United States of America. He settled in Philadelphia and set up a commercial architectural practice in 1870, before spending two years from 1877 travelling in Europe, finally settling back in the UK, in the Surrey and Middlesex area, in 1880. In 1876 there was an international exhibition at Fairmont Park, Philadelphia celebrating the centenary of the founding of the USA. There was demand for images of what the fair would look like and Sydney obliged with a Bird's Eye View print based on drawings of the architects and engineers of the U.S. Commission. The view looks over the fairground from the west with Sydney adding throngs of visitors on all the boulevards and river boats.

In 1875 he married Jane Croucher (born Ramsgate in 1846, dying in 1926), producing three children: Margaret Jane (born in Philadelphia in 1876); Dorothy Isabel (born in 1881, becoming an artist and marrying Captain Benjamin Biggar of the Royal Artillery in Surrey in 1915); Robert Sydney (born in 1883, trained to be an engineer and died in Richmond, Surrey in 1926). Sydney died in June 1912 at 6 St John's Road, Richmond, Surrey, leaving an estate valued at £19,235. Probate was granted to his widow, his son-in-law Benjamin Biggar and a solicitor, William Charles Beasley Robinson.

Three other sons pursued naval or military careers, at least initially. Second son Robert entered the Royal Navy as a teenager but died aged 15 from his injuries after falling from the foretop of HMS Leopard, at that time off Belize. The ship's captain praised Robert for *his amiable qualities and steady attention to his duties* (*The Times*, 21 May 1858).

Berkeley Square where the Smirkes lived and he had his office a few doors along

Third son Albert John joined the United States Army aged 19 in 1863, during the American Civil War. While he died in Hackney, London in 1904, he seems to have spent much time abroad. Becoming a freemason in 1871 at the Prince of Wales Lodge, Jersey he was a beneficiary of his father's will to the extent of £5,000 consols, suggesting his bachelor life travelling did not lend itself to more substantial provision by his father as we shall see below when considering the full details of Smirke's Will.

The fourth son, Edward, settled in the London area (except for a spell at Ventnor, Isle of Wight at the time of the 1881 census) without a profession, successive census returns describing him either as an annuitant or living on means. But he did marry – Henrietta Maria Robinson on 7 August 1878 at Holy Trinity, Bessborough Gardens, London - and had two sons and two daughters.

At the age of 15, fifth son Alfred tried for a naval cadetship but in 1869 switched to the military, purchasing a commission as a cornet in the 1st Dragoons, soon transferring to the 15th Hussars where he spent the remainder of his army career, retiring on a gratuity as a Captain in 1882. Much of his service was spent in India and seeing action in the 2nd Anglo-Afghan War of 1878-79. In 1887 he married Sarah Jane Adams but without issue, living in the Kew area of London. It appears he pursued an active social life attending balls and sporting events. The years 1891 and 1892 were occupied by circumnavigating the world aboard the steam yacht St George, a ship of the Royal Yacht Squadron (Chapter 10 describes this in more detail).

Smirke's and Isabella's three daughters also had contrasting lives and are described in the later section on life in Tunbridge Wells when their major life events occurred. Of Smirke's and Isabella's ten children, just four went on to have twelve children between them. Isabella died before any of her grandchildren had been born, and Smirke only knew of three, one living in the USA and then Europe, one in the north east of England and one in Feltham, Middlesex.

7. Town Planning and Water Supplies

From at least the 1830s, a growing number of professionals, philanthropists, and politicians (both local and national) were increasingly concerned about the Condition of England question, in particular in the rapidly growing industrial and commercial towns and cities. Health and sanitary conditions were of particular concern given the recurring outbreaks of fatal diseases such as cholera and diphtheria and the ever prevalence of tuberculosis. Architects and town planners had a part to play in improving the infrastructure to alleviate rampant infant mortality and early deaths generally. In 1850, the average survival age at birth was 40 for men and 42 for women, with 25% of children dying before the age of five. Yet those surviving childhood had an average life expectancy of 57. By 1900, the average life expectancy at birth had shown modest improvement, to 45 (men) and 55 (women).

Dispensing Water Fun 1860

Town planning was a major area in which Smirke was engaged. A significant set of proposals set out early in his professional life, published in 1834, were his suggestions for the architectural improvement of the western part of London. This was just at the time when the Houses of Parliament had been largely destroyed by fire and national discussion as to a replacement. 93 sets of proposals were submitted, including probably one by Smirke, but Charles Barry (assisted in the execution by A W N Pugin) won the contract.

Smirke produced many plans and drawings to illustrate his thoughts which encompassed Rochester Row, Pall Mall, Haymarket, Leicester Square, St Martin's Lane, the eastern end of Oxford Street and the area south of Lincolns Inn Fields and up to Waterloo Bridge. He noted that, with few exceptions, *the principal avenues of London are such as they were nearly two centuries ago, whilst the population which frequents them has become more than three times as numerous...that a large portion of the west end of London is covered by houses built long before the existence of the present Building Act, and that they are, consequently, precarious properties, requiring a higher insurance, a greater annual expenditure in repairs, and therefore commanding a lower rent than houses of a more recent date and better construction.* He was under no illusion that change would not be easy as he observed opposing interests and clamorous objections. Furthermore, he took the view that London's architectural merit was inferior to many of the continental capitals, that *the standard of public taste is lower in England than in some parts of the continent must probably be concluded.* He went on to refer to the incompetencies of English manufacturers regarding the arts of design, patterns, carpets, cotton, silk, paper hangings and furniture, the *poverty of decorative design.* Slow progress with our *national museums and galleries and the inadequate funds destined for their completion and their support, are proofs of the same tasteless habits, of the same insensibility to the attraction of a refined and rational pleasure. It was humiliating to contrast our parsimonious tardiness in this respect with the bold munificence of other countries.*

His later views on water supply and hygiene were presaged in this 1834 set of proposals as he noted the poorer London districts were *scarcely ever free from the affliction of some malignant and contagious disease... the ill-ventilated and squalid abodes of poverty in those neglected quarters were uniformly the scenes of its earliest appearance, and of its most destructive ravages.* He called for these areas of poverty to be improved, replaced with wider streets *diluting the noxious miasmata, by the injection of a purer atmosphere* by removing old, decayed houses the *hotbeds for the grout of vermin and disease* and by providing complete and effectual drainage.

He put forward many suggestions for improvements in the West End, not least recognising the need for improvements to academic and artistic institutions with which he subsequently became involved: that the new King's College will need to expand, that the Royal Society was constrained within its inadequate physical limits and that the Antiquarian societies had to resort to refusing many contributions owing to a shortage of space and the struggles of the Geological Society to find room for its rapidly increasing collection. As to Westminster Abbey, he suggested the old, worm-eaten timber and brick building leaning against the walls of the Chapter House and the South Transept are taken away *no longer to defile the presence of the sacred edifice and to endanger its security.* Similarly, legal and other public records *which have no general place of deposit, but which are reported by the Record Commission to be rotting in one place, exposed to fire in another and inaccessibly situated in a third* needed a new home. He finished his proposals noting the gradual exclusion of public sculpture and the lack of a decent necropolis in various spots, asking *where are the tombs of our heroes and statesmen?*, noting the mean display of monumental relics in Westminster Abbey and echoing the familiar sayings of the most renowned men of antiquity *that they never gazed upon the sculptured forms of their ancestors without feeling themselves deeply moved to emulate their virtues.*

His ideas foreshadowed many improvements in the London infrastructure of the mid-19th century, especially the groundbreaking sewer constructions devised by Sir Joseph Bazalgette in the 1860s, the rehousing of the poor, influencing social reformer Edwin Chadwick's 1842 report which lead to "Model Houses for Families" designed in the late 1840s by Henry Roberts, a fellow pupil of Sir Robert Smirke.

Smirke's position on water supply and sanitation was captured in his communication (*On Water Supply to Towns*) read at an ordinary general meeting of RIBA on February 22, 1858 (*RIBA Transactions 1857-8*). It follows the premise similarly taken regarding public health provision in municipal areas, that while the rich and comfortably off can make their own arrangements, lack of clean water, adequate sanitation and available health care in the general population can also adversely affect the better off as disease spreads without regard to social status or wealth. (That is not to say that some Victorians sought improvement in the physical and general wellbeing of the less fortunate, also seen as a moral duty.) Early Victorian water companies in London, for example, only supplied well-to-do customers who could afford the plumbing necessary to connect their houses to the main supply. The rest had to make do with a communal tap (if not just rainwater and a local pump) and even then, did not have the time to reach all the water they needed and had no cisterns in which to store it. Despite improvements made arising from the Metropolitan Water Act of 1852, this was not good enough, allowing Lord Shaftesbury, as late as 1871 to comment: *There was scarcely a pint of water in London which was not distinctly unhealthy, and ... a great deal was positively unsafe.* And as we contemplate the state and supply of water in the third decade of the twenty-first century, we may recall the view of many MPs such as Joseph Chamberlain in the 1870s that private management of the water supply was incompatible with public morality: that the supply of water to the poor was *not a legitimate source of profit.*

In his communication, Smirke starts by stating that the issue of water supply *a humble, indeed most unattractive and most anaesthetic, yet a subject which, being of great economic and sanitary importance to the public, need not be unworthy of the attention of any man, still less of the Institute of British Architects.*

He continues: *In very few large towns are the inhabitants able to indulge in the use of an unlimited quantity of water. The wasteful, and indeed, dishonest practices of many often preclude this indulgence, even when the natural supplies of water do not set a limit on its use.* He described how in London the service of water is necessarily confined to a short period and that daily it becomes a matter of great importance to provide each dwelling with receptacles large enough to meet all the reasonable wants of a family for at least twenty-four hours. He noted that such receptacles are far too scanty and sometimes wholly wanting. His solution is to replace the current either inadequate (water butts, lead cisterns) or expensive (slate cisterns) arrangements with *cisterns of a strong, coarse, earthenware, of ample size and at a very low price.* He expected households to pay only modest water rates and noted how one London water company was able to supply a thousand gallons for sixpence, and that on that basis *it was thirty-four times cheaper than a single pint of poor, unwholesome beer.* He called for new building regulations making the supply of water to all houses compulsory, just as the provision of drains had become compulsory. Smirke concluded that *the larger a city becomes, and the greater the aggregation of its inhabitants, the more urgent becomes the duty of the legislature (I say it with great deference) to provide, by stringent measures, and by a vigilant control, for the health and wellbeing of the people.*

His interest in cemeteries was demonstrated by professional involvement in the expansion of Brookwood Cemetery in the age of the railway. Brookwood was opened in 1854 with a private railway terminus being constructed near Waterloo Station at a cost of £23,000 to a design by Tite and W. Cubitt. In keeping with prevailing Victorian class structures, these trains contained passenger carriages reserved for the different classes and Hearse Carriages for the coffins were also arranged by class. These trains came into the cemetery on its dedicated branch line from the adjoining Southwestern Main Line. Together with William Broderick Thomas, Smirke busied himself designing the detailed and extensive evergreen planting scheme. Smirke also designed the two stations in the cemetery itself (one for Anglicans, one for others) while the station builders Messrs Lucas also erected the chapels. Brookwood Necropolis Station was constructed in 1864 and still stands today although Smirke's stations in the cemetery grounds have since been demolished. His work at Brookwood, together with the circular reading room at the British Museum and his Horticultural Society's Galleries in Kensington were described by architectural historian, J Mordaunt Crook, as illuminating *central themes of Victorian culture: the prestige of learning, the cult of nature and the obsession with death.*

Brookwood Cemetery
courtesy of Robert Friedus
Brookwood Cemetery
Victorian Web

8. Later Career and Academic Duties

Later major commissions granted to Smirke were the restoration of the Savoy Chapel, London (1864) – he was Surveyor-General to the Duchy of Lancaster, owners of the Savoy estate then as today - and the exhibition galleries at Burlington House (1868).

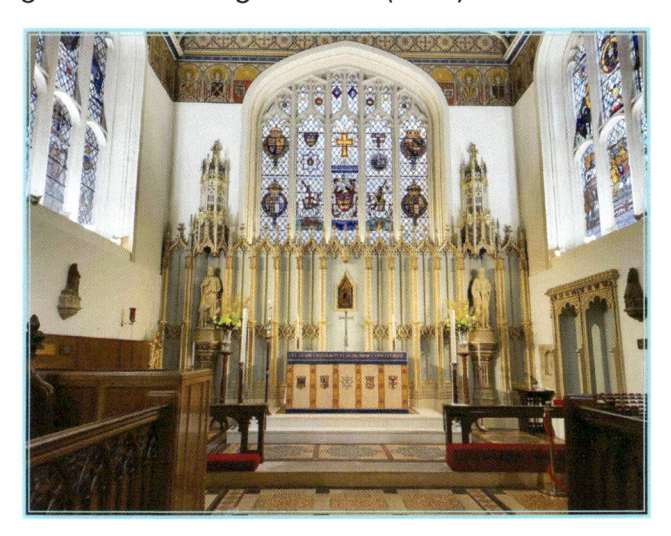

King's Chapel Savoy altar reredos

King's Chapel Savoy font

In 1870 he returned to the Temple site, having previously worked with Decimus Burton on the restoration of the Temple Church, to design the Hall of the Inner Temple. All had benefitted from earlier work carried out by his brother, Sir Robert. But while he never quite acquired a knighthood unlike his brothers Robert and Edward, he did, unlike brother Robert, achieve academic distinction by being elected to the Professorship of Architecture at the Royal Academy in 1861, a post he held until 1865. His lectures were, however, considered uninspiring, although popular. He also served as the Academy's Treasurer between 1861 and 1874.

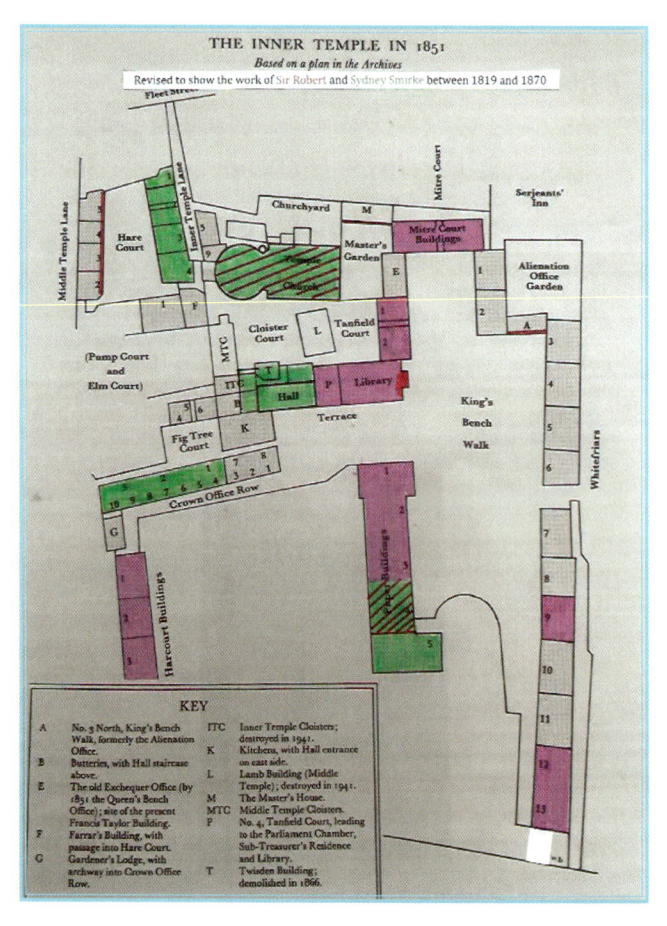

Smirkes Inner Temple plan 1851 courtesy of Inner Temple

Inner Temple New Hall Illustrated London News 12 Feb 1870 ILNHist Archive Gale

A year before his election to the professorship, Smirke became a Royal Gold Medallist (for the promotion of Architecture) of the Royal Institute of British Architects, following in the footsteps of his brother. Indeed, Sir Robert was not well enough to receive his own medal in April 1853 and sent Smirke on his behalf, writing in acknowledgement of *the honour conferred upon him by the award of the Royal Gold Medal, and his gratification at receiving such an expression of the favourable opinion of the Members of the Institute.* In 1860 (March 5 from his home in Cheltenham to which he had recently retired), Sir Robert wrote to congratulate his brother: *If I could have written before without much inconvenience I should have told you how much pleasure it had given me to know that the gold medal of the Institute had been awarded to you. On several occasions I have not thought very favourably of their proceedings and therefore I am the more pleased to know, that in this matter they have, as I think, done what is right.*

As could be expected from a man of his position, there is evidence of attendance at Court and other London social or professional events. *The Times* reported (12 July 1870) that a public meeting would be held the following day at the Mansion House for the exploration and furtherance of the scheme for completing the interior of St Paul's Cathedral left unfinished by Sir Christopher Wren. Chaired by the Lord Mayor of London, the gathering included members of the executive committee set up to complete the work, comprising clergy, politicians and architects including Smirke, George Gilbert Scott and George Richmond. Three years earlier, on 19 June 1867, Smirke had been one of around two hundred guests at a banquet held in the Egyptian Room at the Mansion House to entertain members of the Royal Academy, headed by the President of the Royal Academy, Sir Francis Grant, and the Archbishop of York. Royalty also visited the Royal Academy on 12 May 1869 to acknowledge recent building additions designed by Smirke, when Queen Victoria, the Prince of Wales, Princess Louise, Prince Arthur and Princess Beatrice went to Burlington House, being received by the Royal Academy President, Sir Francis Grant and other Fellows. The Lord Chamberlain, Viscount Sydney, was also in attendance and presented Smirke to Her Majesty.

Family pride was exhibited at the Queen's Levee (taken by the Prince of Wales on Her Majesty's behalf) held at St James' Palace on 31 May 1875 when, as reported in the *Kent & Sussex Courier* four days later, Lieut. Alfred Smirke of the 15th Hussars, was presented by his father, Sydney Smirke.

Smirke's philanthropy and advice on practical matters also featured publicly from time to time. A good example, as reported in the *Kentish Gazette* on 26 December 1876, was reference to a letter to *The Times* written by Smirke concerning fire in theatres. He wrote: *The accounts of the sad fire at the Brooklyn Theatre, Philadelphia have brought to my recollection that I once read a letter from Sir Humphrey Davy to John Ph. Kemble, written at the time when the late Covent Garden Theatre was being built. He suggested that the side canvas screens should be protected from fire by tin-foil secured to the edges where most exposed to accidental contact with the side lights. At the present season, where scenery is being prepared for the Christmas spectacles, some such measure might tend to prevent accidents from fire and consequent panics.* Smirke's public interventions of this nature stretched back many years such as in August 1852 when he commented on the accidental death of a railway passenger by a blow to the head when looking out of a carriage window. While the Board of Trade report into the incident and inquest both blamed the South-Eastern Railway for not barring up carriage windows, Smirke's view was that *the error is in the position of the iron pillars which should never be placed where it was the almost universal custom of railway station builders to place them – viz at the very verge of the platform.*

Smirke's Tunbridge Wells benevolence was noted in the *Kent & Sussex Courier* in 1873 and 1874. In the former year, on 12 and 13 November, the Tunbridge Wells Amateur Dramatic Club gave entertainments at the Great Hall on behalf of the Convalescent Home for Children, even laying on a special train to leave Tunbridge Wells for Tonbridge each evening at the close of the performance. The events were under the *distinguished patronage* of the Earl of Abergavenny, the Hon F G Molyneux, Sir Walter Stirling, Bart., Sir John Briggs, Julian Goldsmid MP and others including Smirke. In 1874 those financially supporting the Tunbridge Wells Royal Parade Subscription Bond were led by well-known local worthies including Mr Brackett, J Delves, Messrs Noakes & Son, Hon F E Molyneux, W Willicombe. Rev R Fowler, Messrs E & H Kelsey, John Colbran, Mrs Cripps and Smirke. Some of these benefactors went on to share Woodbury Park Cemetery as their final resting place.

Casual donations noted in *The Times* included fifteen shillings by Mrs Smirke to the sufferers arising from the explosion caused by the Fenian outrage in Clerkenwell on 13 December 1867. Perhaps this event had for her echoes of the explosion that killed her young brother back in 1854. The Irish Republican Brotherhood, nicknamed the "Fenians", exploded a bomb to try to free one of their members being held on remand at Clerkenwell Prison. The explosion damaged nearby houses killed 12 people and caused 120 injuries. None of the prisoners escaped. The event was described by *The Times* the following day as *a crime of unexampled atrocity* and later described as the most infamous action carried out by the Fenians in Britain in the 19th century. It enraged the public, causing a backlash of hostility in Britain which undermined efforts to establish home rule or independence for Ireland.

Smirke, alongside other RIBA members, was noted as a supporter of the Palestine Exploration Fund whose secretary, Sir George Grove (of Grove's Music fame), thanked supporters, in particular *calling attention to the very hopeful movement among the Freemasons, whose contributions have already reached a highly satisfactory amount.*

Clerkenwell bombing house of detention

The Palestine Exploration Fund was founded under royal patronage in 1865 by a group of distinguished academics and clergy. The original mission statement of the PEF was to promote research into the archaeology and history, manners and customs and culture, topography, geology and natural sciences of biblical Palestine and the Levant. It continues its work today, based in Greenwich, London.

Another institution supported by Smirke was the Female School of Art, founded in 1842 as an adjunct to Somerset House. Run by male governors who considered the students should learn more practical skills to earn a living, to complement those undertaken by working men, this was not the focus of the female principal who wished to attract middle class women who had been left unprovided for and who wished to study the finer arts with a view to making a living as private teachers. This led to the school's expulsion in 1848 to undesirable premises above a soap dealer's shop in The Strand which Charles Dickens described (in *Household Words,* March 1851): *If a paternal Government had studied to select one of the worst possible places for such a school, they could not have more completely succeeded...as to the suitability of its localityfor respectable young females, I may...venture to state...that it is in the close vicinity of several gin-shops, pawn-shops, old rag and rascality shops, in some of the worst courts and alleys of London.* The school subsequently moved to Gower Street in 1852 but the loss of its £500 annual subsidy from the government in 1860 led to a campaign to maintain its financial viability. Moving to Queen's Square a year later, a fund raising conversazione was held on 21 June 1860 at the South Kensington Museum and over £900 was raised by this event and, as noted in *The Times* of 4 July 1860, by individual donations from well-known social campaigners such as F D Maurice (£2) and Louisa Twining (1 guinea) with Smirke donating 3 guineas. Another thousand pounds was sought to ensure the school's long-term future. With royal patronage from 1862 this was secured, and eventually was subsumed into the Central St Martin's College of Art and Design, now the University of the Arts, London.

Royal Female School of Art Life Class 1868

Smirke's major benevolence was closer to home, as the founding president of the Architects' Benevolent Society in 1852, remaining active in that role until his death. His brother Sir Robert was one of two patrons and brother Edward was the Honorary Consulting Counsel. The purpose of the Society – as with many others for different trades and professions – was to give financial support to architects fallen on bad times or their dependants where the breadwinner had died. Amongst the many subscribers were major contributions from the Smirke brothers and from their brother-in-law, John Dobson of Newcastle.

He also served on the boards of a couple of insurance companies: the Architects', Engineers' and Builders' Fire & Life Insurance Company (based at 69 Lombard Street, London) and the British Assurance 2 King's Street, Cheapside, London.

9. Folkestone

Smirke's connections with the Folkestone area stretched over several years. The owner of a large estate of land abutting the small town of Folkestone, Lord Radnor, had a desire to develop it and with the coming of the railway to the town, more possibilities emerged such as development as a seaside resort and an attractive residence for the middle classes. Hitherto Folkestone had been home mainly to fishermen and their families and a few smugglers. By 1845 he had called in Smirke to put forward plans to develop his Folkestone estate. Smirke published a prospectus promoting the virtues of Folkestone and the opportunities for building in the area: *The genius of Steam, that has already effected so many extraordinary social changes in this country, has been peculiarly active here. A few years ago this small, secluded town lay unfrequented and little known…We find it now with a Railway direct to London, a capacious Harbour for large ships, a fine stone pier, and an Hotel with a hundred beds…This change in the character of Folkestone has been so wonderfully rapid, that we find it now almost without a house to receive a visitor.* Designs by Smirke in 1849 resulted in expansion of the shopping area, in Tontine Street and more of his plans that year set out proposals for a major development of residences and facilities to the west of the town. This materialised as The Leas, Sandgate Road and the West Cliff Estate. The Radnor estate had also commissioned Smirke to construct a toll house on the Lower Sandgate Road. This building remains intact, a private residence since 1980, only seven years after the estate stopped taking tolls owing to the lack of traffic. In 1850 Smirke designed and supervised the building of Christ Church (owing to German bombing only the tower remains today set in a small remembrance garden), and an associated national school two years later. New roads with substantial houses emerged in Bouverie Road East and West, with a square and side roads. The Folkestone Improvement Act of 1855 allowed the local authority to extend the limits of the borough, to make new streets, widen existing ones together with other improvements such as town lighting, paving and drainage. As early as 1849, one year after its foundation, Smirke was chairman of the board of directors of the Folkestone Waterworks Company, noting his close interest in water and sanitation issues so eloquently expressed in his later address to RIBA.

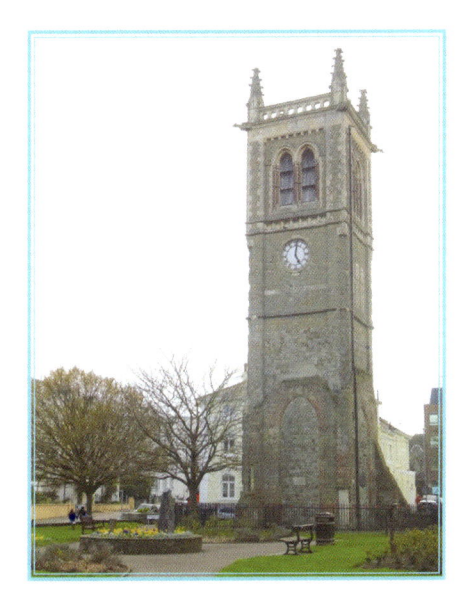

Smirke Toll House front

Christ Church Clock Tower

Smirke's interest in Folkestone continued until the early 1870s. The 1851 census tells us that two of his sons – Robert and Albert – boarded at a small school in the village of Foord, now a suburb of Folkestone. The school – in Brierley Cottage – contained 12 pupils between the ages of four and ten under the ownership of 38-year-old Margaret Donald, assisted by two teenage female assistants, a cook and a housemaid. Little else is apparent about the schooling of Smirke's many children although the boys tended to enter apprenticeships, naval or military training at an early age as was customary at the time.

While having moved from London to Tunbridge Wells by 1870, Smirke and his wife were staying in Folkestone in August 1871 when, aged just 50, Isabella died on the 27th of that month at 37 Sandgate Road. Cancer was the cause of death and one can speculate that sea air was preferred for her final weeks or it might have been coincidence that they were there given Sydney's close association with the town and the work he had undertaken over many years. Earlier in the year, at the time of the 1871 census, they were visitors in Hastings. The death was just seven weeks after the marriage of her eldest daughter which is described in the next section. Isabella's funeral took place at Folkestone's medieval parish church of St Mary's and St Eanswyth and burial in the Cheriton Road Cemetery (section 18 plot C1117). The tomb is inscribed: *Here lies the body of Isabella the dearly loved wife of Sydney Smirke, RA, died August XXVII MDCCCLXXI.* Reports of her death included one in the *Newcastle Courant* (Sept 1, 1871) eldest daughter of the late John Dobson, architect of this town.

St Mary and St Eanswythe high altar Folkestone

Isabella Smirke's death certificate

10. Tunbridge Wells

While not fully retired, Smirke chose to base himself in Tunbridge Wells in 1870, taking up residence at The Hollies, Frant Road (today, Holly Mansions, 20 Frant Road). The Hollies was built in 1868 around the time of the Broadwater Down mansion house development by builder George Mansfield who worked for the landowner developing the area, William, the ageing Fourth Earl of Abergavenny. The Earl died later that year with his son – subsequently advanced to a Marquessate – continuing his development in the area. Smirke's arrival in Tunbridge Wells was at a time of a local sanitation crisis whereby the Court of Chancery had recently found against the Tunbridge Wells Local Commissioners Board (the forerunner of the Town Council) and whose subsequent failure to solve the sanitation problem resulted in the Court of Chancery imposing a sequestration order on the town's assets and revenues, which whilst swiftly suspended, was not removed until 1872 when new local sewage works were certified as adequate. This improvement was largely down to the town's newly appointed surveyor and engineer, William Brentnall, who arrived in Tunbridge Wells in 1870, holding the post almost to his death in 1894. It can be surmised that Smirke would have taken a close interest in these developments given his interest in public health issues.

The Hollies, 20 Frant Road

Not the first owner of The Hollies but nearly so, Smirke took up residence and proceeded to plan an extension to the house, adding a triple storey to one side, with balcony and verandah. Two years later he added a potting and toolshed at the bottom of his long garden. After Smirke's death in 1877, the building remained as a sole residence until 1923 when Thomas Bates and Sons, well known Tunbridge Wells builders, acquired the house and converted it into four apartments. By 1970 Holly Mansions had been divided into eight flats, as it remains today.

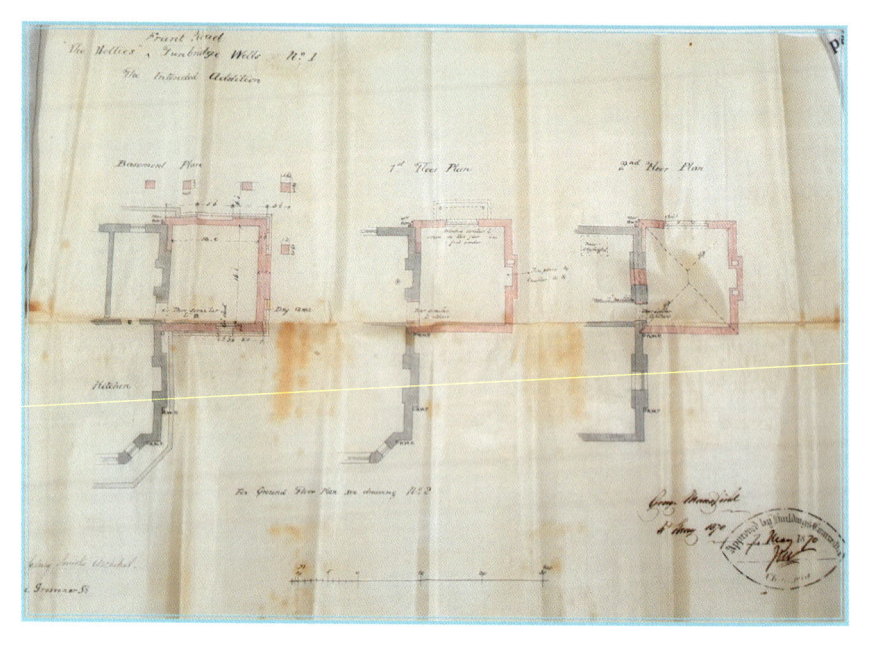

Smirke Hollies 3 floor plan

As we have seen earlier, Smirke was widowed in 1871 but a few weeks earlier, on 5 July, eldest daughter Isabella married William James Montague Lange at St Mark's church, Broadwater Down, Tunbridge Wells. He originated from the north-east of England, West House, Whitburn, County Durham where he was H.M.'s Netherlands Consul at Newcastle upon Tyne and later became a magistrate. Emphasising both families' connection to knights of the realm, the *Morning Post* report on 7 July 1871 noted that the bridegroom was accompanied by his brother, Sir David Adolphus Lange and that after the ceremony the wedding party proceeded to Smirke's residence at The Hollies, Frant Road, where Sir Edward Smirke and other members of the family partook of breakfast. In the afternoon the newly married couple left on their wedding tour.

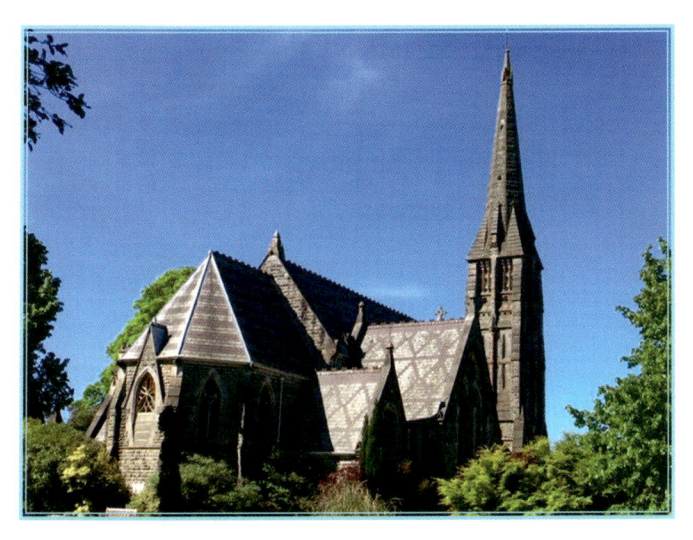

St Marks' Tunbridge Wells

The marriage was not a success and the 1881 census reveals that Isabella was living with her surviving sister and brother-in-law while William remained in the northeast, with their only child, William James Lange, born in 1873 but who died in Monaco only 16 years later. In a Deed of Separation between Isabella and William, dated 6 February 1882, brother Alfred Smirke acted as intermediary to ensure both parties adhered to the separation conditions which would cease on either reconciliation or divorce. The agreement provided that Isabella may live a separate life and from control of William Lange and he cannot cohabit, molest or interfere with her. Arrangements were made for their only child, nine-year-old William, in that he would reside with his father in County Durham when not at boarding but that he could reside with his mother during the last 14 days of January, the first 14 days of July and for seven days from Maundy Thursday. Isabella was also to have free access to her son, whether at school or elsewhere except the residence of her husband, while both parents may have access should the child be ill.

Smirke and two daughters

Two years later, tragedy struck the Smirke household again when Smirke's youngest daughter, Margaret Jane, died on 29 November 1873 aged only 19. The cause of death was typhoid fever and pneumonia. Whilst she had moved to Tunbridge Wells, her place of death was 14, Cannon Place, Brighton. This perhaps illustrates the popularity of seaside resorts for the ailing, just as inland spas such as Tunbridge Wells had fulfilled that role in generations past yet still attracting the infirm and retiring.

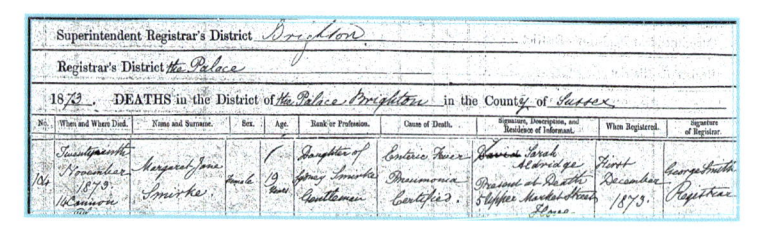

Margaret Jane's death certificate

Wedding bells rang again for the Smirke family at St Mark's, Tunbridge Wells, this time for daughter Mary Octavia, who was married there by its Vicar, Revd Frederick Richard Johnstone, on 25 November 1874. Her husband had been its curate, the Revd John Francis Jemmett (1848-1926). After another curacy in Tring, by 1877 he had settled into his lifelong incumbency as Vicar of St Dunstan's Feltham, Middlesex where they raised their three daughters (Mary Kate, Violet Octavia and Winifred Sheila) and one son (Frank Rupert). Mary survived her husband by 18 years, dying on 9 June 1944, buried at Warminghurst, near Horsham, West Sussex.

Jemmett was not a poor clergyman but came from a wealthy and well-connected family. His father, a London merchant, had held the patronage of the Feltham incumbency but this had been sold to George Wythes more recently. The Wythes had family seats at Bickley Hall, near Bromley, Kent and Copped Hall, near Waltham Abbey, Essex. George's son and heir, George Edward Wythes had, in 1866, married Jemmett's sister, Catherine Sarah in Kingston upon Thames. George Wythes snr had made a fortune in the construction of railways and as a developer in furnaces and mining. His railway construction was not only relatively local – the Essex line and the Brighton to Shoreham line - but more significantly in Argentina, South Africa and in building the Great Indian Peninsula Railway. It was said that there were few countries in Europe with which his name and capital were not associated, and that he had property scattered over almost every quarter of the globe. It was George Edward Wythes' and his wife Catherine Sarah's son and heir, Ernest Wythes who financed and sailed around the world in 1891-92 in the Royal Yacht Squadron St George. Three of his gentlemen companions were Christ Church Oxford contemporaries and another was Smirke's son, Captain Alfred Smirke. An account of the voyage was written by the ship's doctor, George Fyfe, MD, where it was stated that the St George *was a three-masted auxiliary-screw steam yacht, and next to the Royal yachts was one of the largest and finest of the Royal Yacht Squadron, built at Leith by Ramage & Ferguson from the design and specifications of a first class yacht architect at a cost of about £50,000.* It had a crew of 37 sailors and officers, nine stewards and seven gentleman travellers. In an account of that near two-year world voyage, Alfred Smirke was described – in the *Sydney Mail* of June 4, 1892 - *as taking a well earned rest after a distinguished service in India.*

Mr Wythes and Friends

Smirke had made financial provision for Isabella and Mary Octavia in anticipation of their respective marriages. This was prudent because safeguards for married women (as opposed to single women and widows who had property rights) over assets on marriage were only achieved piecemeal, early progress coming with the Married Women's Property Act of 1870 but fuller protection not achieved until after the Acts of the same name passed in 1882 and 1884.

He covenanted to pay £200 per annum via two trustees to each *daughter for her sole and separate use independently of the said (named husband to be) and of his debts or interference so that her receipts alone shall be discharged and she shall not have power to deprive herself of the benefit by any alienation or anticipations thereof.* The covenant for Isabella Smirke was dated 5 July 1871 showing Smirke resident at Grosvenor Street, Grosvenor Square, London, and two trustees, his son Edward, based in the Hollies, Frant Road, Tunbridge Wells and Thomas Lambert of 26 St George's Place, Canterbury. Lambert (1825-1905) was married to Laura, only child of Smirke's older brother Sir Robert Smirke. Son of Admiral Sir George Robert Lambert, he had been a Captain in the Royal Artillery and was a magistrate. In 1867, he and his wife donated to the Tate Gallery a series of paintings by Smirke's father, Robert Smirke, on themes around Don Quixote. The covenant for Mary Octavia was dated 24 November 1874 with Sir Edward Smirke as a trustee alongside Thomas Lambert.

Whilst remaining based in Tunbridge Wells, Smirke continued to take commissions and an active interest in national and current affairs. A major commission in 1872 was his second set of works at Burlington House, Piccadilly. Originally a Restoration House of the 1660s, Burlington House was transformed by Colen Campbell into a Palladian palace between 1717 and 1720, sympathetically remodelled by Samuel Ware between 1815 and 1818 and altered and enlarged by Smirke in 1868 by the addition of the exhibition rooms and between 1872 and 1874 he added a third storey to the building. Between his new Corinthian columns were placed 19th century statues of famous artists such as Leonardo da Vinci, Raphael, Michelangelo, Titian, Sir Joshua Reynolds and Sir Christopher Wren. A review of Smirke's work by Walter Ison in *The Apollo* magazine of January

Burlington House Third Floor

1969 was not complimentary: *Sydney Smirke's additions of 1872-74 were disastrous in their effect on Campbell's well proportioned and finely detailed front. Despite the appropriate use of a Corinthian order and adherence to Campbell's system of bay spacing, Smirke's loftly and over-ornamented upper story has had a most depressing effect on Campbell's Ionic piano mobile. This is made worse by its partial concealment behind the balustrade above the rusticated Doric arcade which Smirke added to form an entrance loggia extending between the projecting wings.*

Smirke died at The Hollies on 8 December 1877, just twelve days short of his 80th birthday. The cause was put down to a hepatic obstruction lasting ten days (obstruction of the hepatic vein prevents blood flowing out of the liver and back to the heart and can cause liver damage). He was buried in Woodbury Park Cemetery with his youngest daughter, Margaret Jane. His Will, dated 12 January 1872, made just after his wife's death but before Margaret Jane's, was proved on 30 January 1878 and reported in *The Times* on 22 February 1878. The executors were Thomas Lambert, Miss Margaret Jane Dobson (sister of his late wife) and Simon Adams Beck with his personal estate not exceeding £80,000. Sydney bequeathed his honorary medals to his daughters for life and then to the President and Council of the Royal Academy *to be preserved by them for ever.* His furniture and household effects were also to pass to his daughters while Simon Beck was to receive £200 per annum for managing his property. Settled on his daughters was a sum to provide each with an annual income of £650 and upon trust for his son Albert John for life, Consuls to the value of £5,000. The rest of his property was left equally to his three surviving sons, Sydney, Edward and Alfred.

Smirke death certificate

In the January following his death, the *Kent and Sussex Courier* (25 January 1878) and the London *Evening Standard* (28 January 1878) advertised an auction of surplus furniture and Landau from The Hollies, Frant Road. The auctioneers were Messrs Glasier and Sons of 41 Charing Cross Road, London. The following description of items gives a flavour of the quality of the contents: *the remainder of well-made furniture and effects, including brass, iron and Mahogany French, Arabian bedsteads, superior bedding, marble-top and other wash stands... fancy tables, brilliant plate chimney glass, mantel clocks, cottage pianoforte in rosewood, mahogany dining room suite, bureau, easy and occasional chairs, oak library table and bookcase, steel and brass mounted fenders, carpets, iron safe, contents of servants' offices and garden effects.*

Of the various notices of Smirke's death, that in *The Times* dated December 12, 1877, described him as *the survivor of a family of distinguished men in the arts...he had travelled much, and his sketch books are full of memoranda of foreign buildings most carefully drawn. He was extremely accurate and emulated the character of his brother, who was considered to have never exceeded his estimate, taking care fully to calculate the probable cost and thus to secure his employers from disappointment or possible embarrassment. He was looked up to by the profession as a most honourable man, amiable in his disposition, somewhat reserved, but valued by all who had the privilege of his acquaintance or friendship.* A later appreciation came from the son of Sir Charles Barry (with whom Smirke had collaborated), quoted in the 1885 book written by Margaret Jane Dobson (Smirke's sister-in-law) setting out memoirs of her father, John Dobson: *Mr Smirke, like a true artist, was sensitive and retiring in manner. He was emphatically a man of honour, possessing a refined taste and cultivated mind; he shrank from all that appeared exaggeration or vulgarity, either in Art or Society.* His life has been well described as that of *a skilful constructor, an accomplished artist and a Christian gentleman.*

Sources

Primary

Census returns

General Register Office

British Newspapers Online

Royal Institute of British Architects Archives (both at RIBA and at the V&A including RIBA Transactions and RIBA Proceedings)

British Library (286 letters from architects, artists and public figures mostly to Sydney Smirke donated by F R Jemmett)

Athenaeum Club archives

Suggestions for the Architectural Improvement of the Western Part of London by Sydney Smirke, Priestley and Weale, London 1834

Extension Plans to The Hollies, Frant Road, Tunbridge Wells, 6 May 1870, TWBC

Memoirs of John Dobson of Newcastle on Tyne – Margaret Jane Dobson – Hamilton Adams and co – 1885

Secondary

Seven Victorian Architects – ed. Jane Fawcett – chapter on Sydney Smirke by J Mordaunt Crook - Thames & Hudson 1976

The History of Folkestone – The Story of a Town – Dr C H Bishop – 1973

Magazines: Apollo; The Builder; Country Life

A few local buildings to visit illustrating Smirke's architectural work

Tunbridge Wells:

- 20 The Hollies, Frant Road (his extension to earlier build)

Folkestone:

- The Toll House, Lower Sandgate Road
- Christ Church Tower, Sandgate Road

London:

- British Museum Reading Room
  (now circular area with enclosed exhibition space)
- Burlington Arcade, Piccadilly
- Savoy/King's Chapel, Savoy Hill, Strand
- Oxford and Cambridge Club, 71 Pall Mall
- Dome Chapel of the Bethlem Royal Hospital
  (now the Imperial War Museum)

Acknowledgements and references

The author is grateful for the encouragement and advice received from June Bridgeman, Ian Beavis, Research Curator, Amelia Scott Centre Tunbridge Wells (extension plans of 20 Frant Road), Jennie De Protani, Archivist, The Athenaeum Club (membership details), Celia Pilkington, Archivist Inner Temple (1851 Temple plans) and Colin Webb for so skilfully formatting the text for printing.

The author and publishers have made every effort to establish the copyright of the illustrations used, including those that can be found on websites, but with no attribution, and apologise for any oversight or omissions.

All proceeds from this booklet go towards the conservation work of the Friends of Woodbury Park Cemetery www.fwpc.org.uk

printed by Laser Repro 2000

Some of our other publications available to order

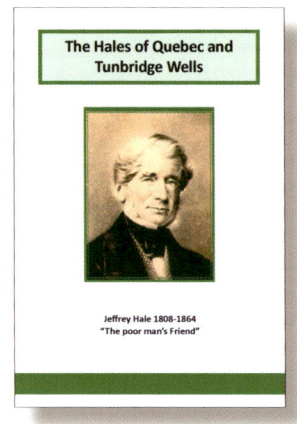

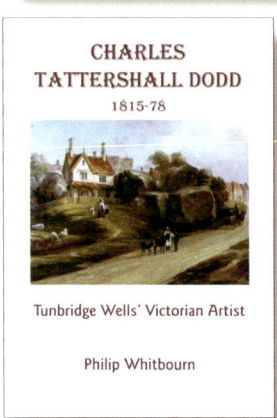

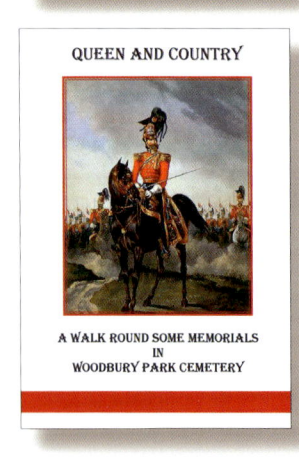

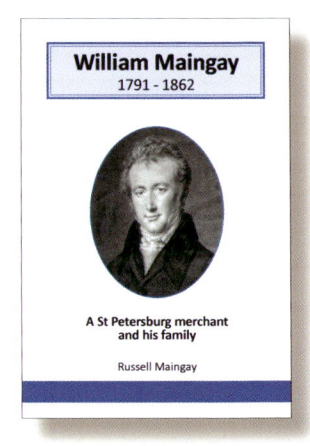

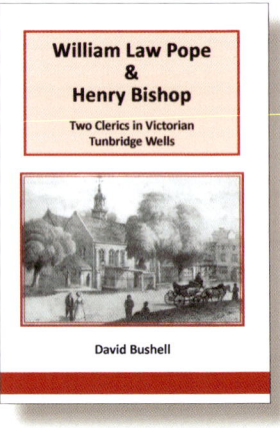

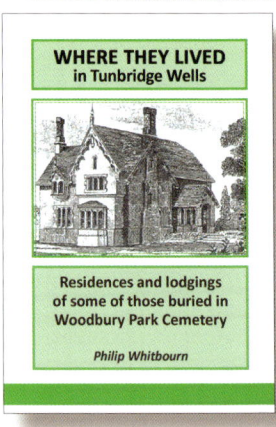

The Hales of Quebec and Tunbridge Wells
Jeffrey Hale 1808-1864
"The poor man's Friend"

William Maingay
1791 - 1862
A St Petersburg merchant and his family
Russell Maingay

CHARLES TATTERSHALL DODD
1815-78
Tunbridge Wells' Victorian Artist
Philip Whitbourn

William Law Pope & Henry Bishop
Two Clerics in Victorian Tunbridge Wells
David Bushell

QUEEN AND COUNTRY
A WALK ROUND SOME MEMORIALS IN WOODBURY PARK CEMETERY

WHERE THEY LIVED in Tunbridge Wells
Residences and lodgings of some of those buried in Woodbury Park Cemetery
Philip Whitbourn